Chinese Goldfish

Chinese Goldfish

Revised Edition   1990

ISBN 7-119-00408-5
Order: 16035

Copyright 1990 by Foreign Languages Press

Published by Tetra Press
201 Tabor Road, Morris Plains, New Jersey 07950

Printed by Toppan Printing Co. (Singapore) Ltd.

Distributed in the United States, Canada,
United Kingdom, and Australia by Tetra Press
201 Tabor Road, Morris Plains, New Jersey 07950

CONTENTS

Goldfish—Flower of the Water

THE goldfish is a traditional Chinese ornamental fish. Because of its gorgeous colours and elegant graceful shape people call it the flower of the water.

Its home is China. Since its domestication in the southern Song Dynasty (1127-1279) the varieties of goldfish have increased continually. Goldfish from China have been introduced directly or indirectly into different countries of the world.

Raising goldfish costs little but brings much pleasure. Goldfish beautify gardens, parks and courtyards. If a few goldfish pools are placed in the midst of flowers and verdant trees, the riot of colours as the goldfish swim and frolic between green grass and bizarre rocks will enliven picturesque scenery. In China goldfish have become an indispensable artistic ornament for beautifying the environment.

Appreciating goldfish has become a favourite pastime, enriching people's aesthetic taste and relaxing the mind. After intense work if one stands quietly beside an aquarium to appreciate beautiful, vivacious goldfish, one will begin to feel carefree and happy, with all fatigue gone.

Goldfish are easy to raise. Since they do not require much equipment or expense, children can also gain a wealth of knowledge from raising goldfish.

The Chinese people love goldfish. In celebration of an excellent harvest and the lunar New Year they usually put up New Year posters of goldfish symbolizing "Surplus in coming years"* and, therefore, happiness and perfect satisfaction. The gorgeous colours and beautiful shapes of goldfish have been used widely in different sorts of plastic and applied arts to enrich people's lives.

Raising a few goldfish will certainly bring you joy and delight.

---

*In Chinese, the character for fish is homonymous with the character for surplus.

1. Variegated butterfly tail.

2. Purple high head.

3. Blue pearl scales.

4. Cinnabar eyes with high head.

Yellow high head.

. Red high head.

7. Red-and-white dragon eyes.

8. Jade-seal impression on head.

9. Black dragon eyes with red head.

10. Egg shape with phoenix tail and crane's red crest.

11.
Front: Red-and-white bubble eyes with hoisted fins.
Rear: Red bubble eyes with hoisted fins.

12. Goldfish gallery in Zhongshan
Park, Beijing.

13. Interior of goldfish gallery in
Hangzhou Zoo.

4. Goldfish gallery in Shanghai Zoo.

5. Exterior of goldfish gallery in Hangzhou Zoo.

16. Porcelain plate with goldfish

17. Goldfish wood carving

18. An ink slab with carved goldfish border designs.

19. Silver jar

20. Lacquer painting with goldfish design.

21. Postage stamps with goldfish designs.

22. New Year woodcut.

23. Goldfish stone carving in Xi'ar Children's Park.

Origin and Development of Goldfish Raising in China

OVER the long course of raising goldfish the Chinese have used an important variation of its ancestor, the orange *ji yu* (crucian carp—*Carassius auratus*), introduced in a new environment to breed many varieties of goldfish through artificial selection. They have stored up a wealth of experience in this work. Crucian carp, a delicious species, is found and eaten everywhere in China. In its natural state it is grey, but an orange one occasionally appears.

Origin and Development of Domestic Goldfish

A thousand or so years ago in the Northern Song Dynasty (960-1127) an orange fish was discovered in Hangzhou and Jiaxing, Zhejiang Province. Its scales shone with golden radiance, gorgeous and dazzling. As it was entirely identical with wild crucian carp, people called it golden crucian carp. At that time people took this beautiful fish as something sacred, and it was prohibited to catch it. Thus golden crucian carp survived peacefully in its natural environment (Figs. 24, 25).

In Southern Song times the royal family built artificial ponds in the gardens of palaces in Lin'-an (present-day Hangzhou), captured golden crucian carp and raised them in ponds. Many high-ranking officials and aristocrats followed suit. They vied with one another in demanding golden crucian carp from different parts of the country and built ponds to breed them. Thus domestication of goldfish began.

To ensure survival of the goldfish, people were appointed at the imperial palaces and in the mansions of high-ranking officials to take charge of raising them. Gradually tending fish became a profession. People found an ideal food—red water fleas in foul water—for goldfish and a method of propagation. Further variation occurred in the colours of goldfish and white and mottled goldfish appeared. The fish also increased enormously in numbers.

In Ming times (1368-1644) medical scientist and pharmacologist Li Shizhen (1518-1593) in his book *Compendium of Materia Medica* (also called, *Outline of Herb Medicine*, published in 1596), a famous work on Chinese medicine and pharmacology, recorded how

widespread the raising of goldfish was at that time: "Some people in Song times began to breed goldfish and now raising them has become a pastime in homes everywhere."

People began raising goldfish in tubs and jars instead of in ponds, since it was more convenient for tending and admiring. As containers became simpler, the raising of goldfish spread widely and took on new dimensions. People carefully selected different kinds of goldfish to hybridize and bred new varieties, such as twin tails, long fins, protruding eyes and short body. At this time Chinese varieties of goldfish and the art of raising them began to spread abroad, introduced first into Japan in 1502.

Detailed accounts of goldfish raising in Ming times appeared in Wang Xiangjin's *A Manual of the Beautiful and Fragrant Flowers of Er'ru Pavilion* which was published in 1630 and contained descriptions of gardening, farming, fish breeding and so forth; *A Brief Account of Scenery and Objects in the Imperial Capital*, written by Liu Tong and Yu Yizheng and published in 1634 describing spots of scenic beauty and historic interest, flowers, trees, insects and fish in and around Beijing; *A Manual of Goldfish*, written by Zhang Qiande and published in 1596, and *Anecdotes of Pastimes*, written by Tu Long and published in 1592. Of these books Zhang Qiande's *A Manual of Goldfish* is a classic work on the Chinese art of goldfish raising and the author has been called the father of fish-raising enthusiasts.

In the Qing Dynasty (1644-1911) goldfish raising became more prevalent. As tastes grew more refined, people realized the necessity of artificial selection in breeding. *Notes About Insects and Fish*, published in 1904, says, "If you want to obtain good varieties, the crux of the matter lies in excellent species of parent fish, which will certainly yield fine fry." With constant improvement in artificial selection and in the art of fish

raising rare varieties were bred, including dragon eyes, lion head, sky-gazing eyes and velvet balls.

The goldfish of Qing times possessed the essential characteristics of modern goldfish with their rich variety of colours and beautiful shapes. People became increasingly interested in goldfish, so that raising

goldfish in courtyards and indoors was a prevailing trend. Books describing methods of raising goldfish, such as *Random Notes in Bamboo Leaves Pavilion*, written by Yao Yuanwen, published in 1893, and *Methods of Raising Goldfish*, written by Bao Shikui, published in 1899, increased. They summed up the experience of raising goldfish and promoted its development. They also accelerated the spread of goldfish abroad. Goldfish were introduced into Britain in 1794 and into the United States in 1878. They spread to different countries of the world early in the twentieth century.

Nevertheless, over a long period goldfish were appreciated by only a small number of people who merely followed previous practice in the art of raising them and did not make innovations, so goldfish raising made very slow progress.

New Developments in Varieties of Goldfish and Scientific Research

Goldfish raising has made rapid progress since the 1950s. The government has allocated funds to build and expand goldfish breeding centres and train large numbers of professional in this field. Meanwhile scientists and technicians have conducted research on raising, tending, preventing disease and breeding, thus creating conditions for scientific raising of goldfish. As a result, raising goldfish in China is on an unprece-

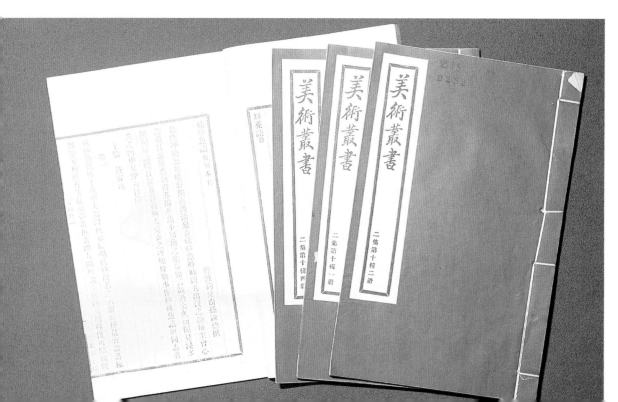

26. Zhang Qiande's *A Manual of Goldfish*, published in 1596.

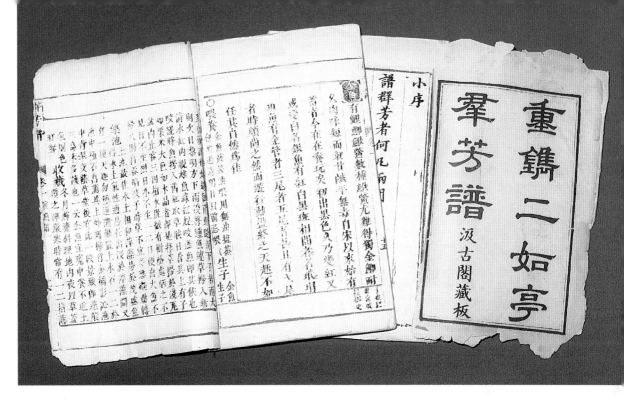

7. Wang Xiangjin's *A Manual of the Beautiful and Fragrant Flowers of 'ru Pavilion*, published in 1630.

...ented scale, having spread to the north and south of ...hina. In the cities especially about one-third of the ...ouseholds raise goldfish, from a few to dozens of fish.

As methods of crossbreeding have been widely ...dopted and various places have bred goldfish for ...ifferent purposes, the varieties of goldfish have mul-...flied. The northern areas, represented by Beijing, ...ress rare attributes of goldfish in breeding. They have ...red a number of rare varieties, including balls with ...eversed gills and dragon eyes; balls with dragon eyes ...nd high head; dragon eyes with reversed gills and ...earl scales; dragon eyes with pearl scales; and purple ...earl scales. The southern areas, represented by Hang-...hou and Shanghai, pay attention to local variations ...n colour as well as variation in shape. They have bred

a number of goldfish varieties, such as sky-gazing bubble eyes, cinnabar eyes and red crest in purple gauze robe, well known at home and abroad. In addition, god of longevity's head, sedate and with natural grace, bred in Guangzhou; variegated pearl scales, with a belly round like a ball, bred in Fuzhou; black butterfly tail, which is as black as traditional Chinese ink, bred in the Yangzhou area, have their own distinctive characteristics. Varieties of Chinese goldfish now number over three hundred thirty.

Goldfish have scientific value too, being good material for biological studies of heredity, evolution and embryogenesis. Chinese biologist Chen Zhen (Shisan C. Chen, 1894-1957) began in the 1920s to

28. Red carplike fish, shaped like the Chinese character 文 (*wen*).

29. Egg shape with red head.

30. Dragon eyes with red head.

study the heredity, evolution and variations of goldfish. He published very valuable writings in this realm that have been highly regarded by Chinese and foreign scientists. Under his influence scientists have paid ever more attention to Chinese goldfish.

Chinese experimental biologist Professor Zhu Xi (1899-1962) utilized goldfish for his study "The Re-

1. Red lion head.

32. Dragon eyes with reversed gills and red pearl scales.

lationship Between the Maturity of Ovum and the Development of Embryo," making an important contribution to studies of Chinese fish. Chinese biologist Professor Tong Dizhou (1902-1979) conducted studies on cytogenetics and achieved gratifying results and a breakthrough in Chinese cytogenetics.

Chinese biologists have also conducted scientific

33. Variegated bubble eyes with hoisted fins.

34. A corner of the fish grounds in Beijing Zoo—goldfish reared in wooden tubs.

35. Exterior of the fish grounds in Beijing Flower and Tree Company.

research on the origin of goldfish. They believe that goldfish and wild crucian carp belong to the same genus and the same species, for the following reasons: 1) Goldfish of any variety can be crossbred with wild crucian carp and produce offspring with normal reproductive capacity. 2) Goldfish and wild crucian carp have the same serum reaction. 3) Cytologically, goldfish and crucian carp are different only in colour and in their behaviour towards humans. The two are very similar in shape in their embryonic and early periods. Evidently, goldfish of every description originate from the offspring of wild crucian carp—the golden crucian carp.

Scientists also believe that although many varieties of goldfish are bred from artificial hybridization, environmental changes are the prime cause of variation in golden crucian carp. After its domestication golden crucian carp at first showed only variation in colour. When tubs and jars were used to raise the fish, the confined space of the containers caused them to swim more and more slowly and to depend on an artificial supply of feed. This has brought about

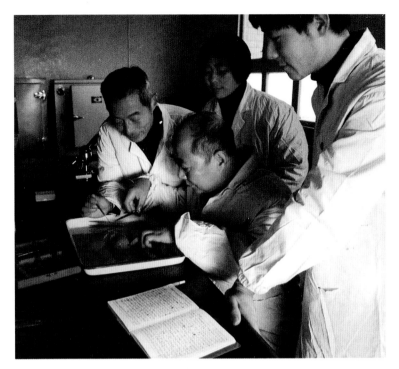

36. Chinese scientists and technicians conducting research on goldfish.

37. On-the-spot observation of the growth of goldfish.

variations in various organs of the goldfish's body. Its long, lean sides have become oval shaped and some dorsal fins have become fragmentary or have vanished. Their caudal fins have also evolved into many shapes because they had to adapt to turning up and down in a small tub. By now goldfish naturally differ greatly from their ancestor, the golden crucian carp. The following Evolution Chart of the Varieties of Goldfish shows how the goldfish family has developed.

A variety in Hangzhou area: gazing red bubble eyes.

9. A variety in Beijing area: Red balls with reversed gills and dragon eyes.

40. A variety in Fuzhou area: Variegated pearl scales.

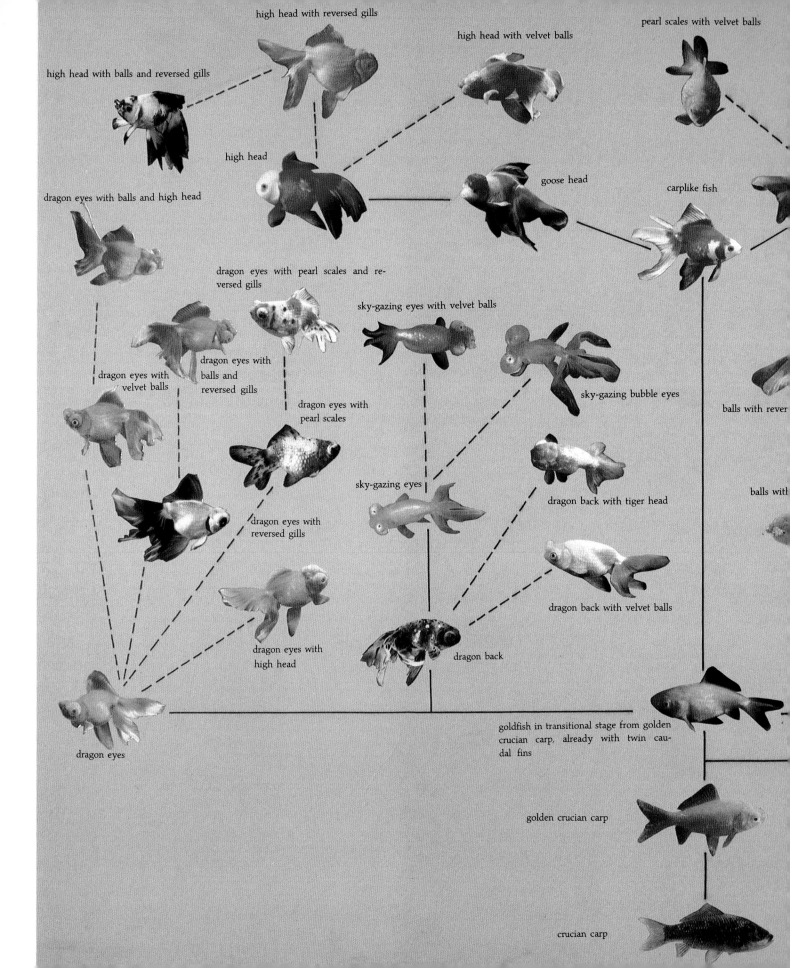

high head with reversed gills

high head with velvet balls

pearl scales with velvet balls

high head with balls and reversed gills

high head

goose head

carplike fish

dragon eyes with balls and high head

dragon eyes with pearl scales and reversed gills

sky-gazing eyes with velvet balls

dragon eyes with balls and reversed gills

dragon eyes with velvet balls

sky-gazing bubble eyes

balls with rever

dragon eyes with pearl scales

balls with

dragon eyes with reversed gills

sky-gazing eyes

dragon back with tiger head

dragon back with velvet balls

dragon eyes with high head

dragon back

goldfish in transitional stage from golden crucian carp, already with twin caudal fins

dragon eyes

golden crucian carp

crucian carp

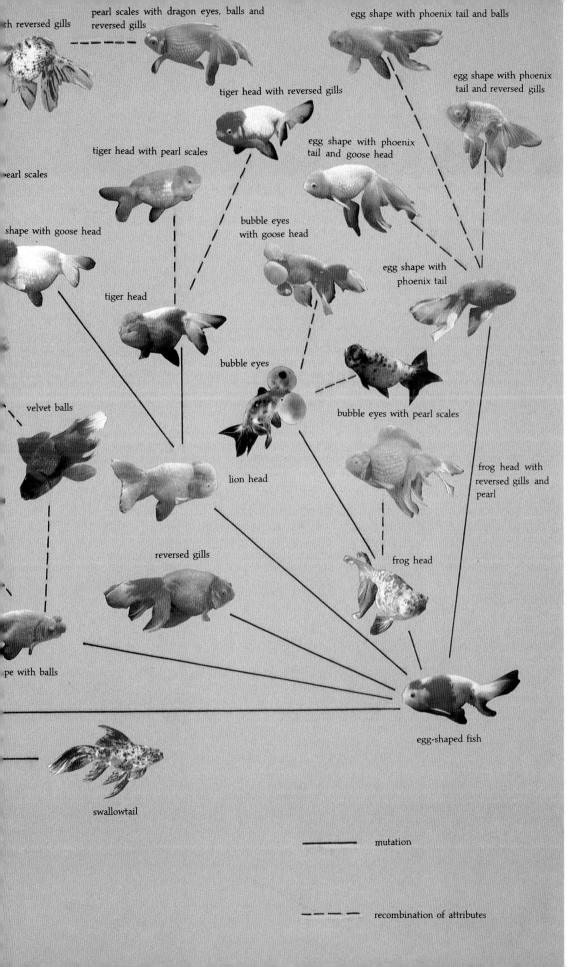

pearl scales with dragon eyes, balls and
reversed gills

h reversed gills

egg shape with phoenix tail and balls

egg shape with phoenix
tail and reversed gills

tiger head with reversed gills

tiger head with pearl scales

egg shape with phoenix
tail and goose head

earl scales

bubble eyes
with goose head

shape with goose head

egg shape with
phoenix tail

tiger head

bubble eyes

velvet balls

bubble eyes with pearl scales

frog head with
reversed gills and
pearl

lion head

reversed gills

frog head

pe with balls

egg-shaped fish

swallowtail

——————— mutation

----------- recombination of attributes

Goldfish can be classified into three major
categories: dragon varieties, egg-shaped
varieties and carplike varieties shaped like
the Chinese character 文(*wen*). Today's
more than three hundred varieties of
goldfish evolved basically from these
three major categories.

Fantastic Shapes and Astonishing Colours

GOLDFISH display their beauty mainly through colour and the shape of their eyes, head and caudal fins. Their colours have a myriad variations. Their eyes are either flat or protruding, each having special charm. Their heads are diverse in shape. Some resemble a brave lion holding its head high; some look like an old woman wearing flowers on her head. When goldfish swim, their gossamerlike caudal fins move lithely through the water. No wonder goldfish have been an object of admiration for Chinese literati for a thousand years.

Astonishing Colours

The rich variety of goldfish colours is enchanting. How are these colours formed? Under the microscope you can see that colours on the goldfish's scales are composed of three substances: melanin, orange-red pigment and light-blue reflective substances. Different combinations of these three substances produce the colours on the goldfish's body.

In the case where melanin has entirely vanished, orange-red pigment and the reflective substance make up the gorgeous red colour. In the case where melanin is very thick, you may see a small amount of orange-red pigment and the light-blue reflective substance in the gaps of melanin, and this is black. Sparkling, lustrous white goldfish have only light-blue reflective substance on their scales. Purple goldfish are that colour because there is less melanin than orange-red pigment on their scales and blue goldfish owe their hue to a deficiency of orange-red pigment.

As various pigments exist simultaneously and are distributed in different proportions, some goldfish possess more than two colours, so there are fantastic variegated, red and white, purple and blue goldfish. Indeed, they are a riot of colour, which is why people call goldfish flowers of the water.

Beautiful Shapes

Goldfish have short, round bodies, large protruding eyes and long or short caudal fins, single or in pairs.

A single caudal fin is identical to that of a crucian

2. Goldfish of fantastic shapes and astonishing colours.

44. Goose head.

43. Fins—butterfly tail.

carp. Double caudal fins, in general, are shaped in two ways: If the two dorsal lobes are linked together but the two abdominal lobes are divided, it is called three caudal fins; if the two dorsal lobes are entirely or partially divided and the two abdominal lobes are also divided, it is called four caudal fins. The four-caudal-fin variety is highly prized (Fig. 43).

45. Tiger head.

46. Lion head.

47. Dragon eyes.

48. Sky-gazing eyes.

49. Bubble eyes.

The goldfish's head can be flat, a lion head, goose head or tiger head. The lion-head variety has a square, helmetlike shape on its crown and substantial bulges all over its head (Fig. 46). The goose-head variety has only a square bulge on the crown (Fig. 44). The tiger-head variety has a layer of evenly distributed bulges covering its whole head and no helmetlike shape on its crown (Fig. 45). The so-called flat head

50. Pearl scales.

is shaped like that of a crucian carp. Other head patterns, such as high head and frog head, are variations of these four basic head patterns.

Goldfish eyes can be classified as dragon, sky-gazing, bubble and normal. Dragon eyes bulge on each of the head (Fig. 47). Sky-gazing eyes protrude and turn upward at a 90-degree angle, the pupils turning skyward (Fig. 48). Bubble eyes have globular translucent tissues under the eye sockets, forcing the pupils to turn skyward and become two bubbles (Fig. 49). Goldfish with normal eyes, similar to those of the crucian carp, have very small pupils.

Goldfish may also have sparkling pearllike scales (Fig. 50), velvet balls swaying with the water (Fig. 53), reversed gills showing bright-red gill filaments (Fig. 51) and a smooth back with no dorsal fin.

51. Reversed gills.

52 High head, balls and dragon eyes.

53. Velvet balls.

Propagation of Goldfish

SPRING, with its warm, sunny days and gentle breezes, is the propagation season for goldfish. Fish more than one year old with mature sex glands can produce. They spawn once a year.

Distinguishing Between Male and Female

Under ordinary circumstances it is difficult to distinguish between male and female goldfish. The sex is shown prominently only during the propagation period. An ancient Chinese book has the following record: "In late winter white spots appear on the gills of male goldfish reared in a tub. Choose males with well-shaped eyes, gills, head and tail and put them in a jar with a female early in spring so that miscellaneous varieties cannot mingle with them." This shows one method for distinguishing the sex of goldfish.

In general, the sex can be distinguished by the following characteristics:

1) "Chasing star" (or pearl organ)—a small white cone-shaped spot. This appears because the goldfish's epidermal tissues are thick and become horny. Under ordinary circumstances the "chasing star" seldom appears. Only in the propagation period do "chasing stars" appear obviously on the gill cover, breast fin and abdominal fin of males. Females have none (Fig. 54).

2) Scales. If you gently press goldfish scales, you'll find that the scales of the male are in overlapping rows, while those of the female are in loose array.

3) Shape of the belly. The male has a long body and a shuttle-shaped belly. There is no apparent boundary line between its belly and its tail. The female has a short body and an oval belly with a distinct boundary line between the belly and the tail.

4) Fin. The male breast fin and abdominal fin are rather hard and it swims fast, while the female has a fairly soft breast fin and always swims slowly.

54. The phenomenon of "chasing star" that appears in male fish during the propagation period.

5) Genital aperture. The male's genital aperture i shuttle shaped; the female's is round and becomes red swollen and bulging in propagation season (Fig. 55)

Conditions for Spawning

Whether or not goldfish propagate well depend directly on external conditions.

Females spawn from March to May every year During this period the weather turns warm and the water temperature is appropriate. When the wate temperature rises to 15 degrees Centigrade, goldfish begin to spawn. If the water temperature suddenly drops below 15 degrees Centigrade, goldfish will stop spawning. Only when the water regains normal temperature, will goldfish continue to spawn. Intensity and duration of sunshine also influence spawning. On rainy days goldfish seldom spawn. Only when the weather is clear and sunshine plentiful will goldfish spawn normally.

Before the goldfish spawn, put male fish and aquatic weeds in the jar prepared for spawning. Male fish stimulate the female fish to spawn early and normally, while aquatic weeds serve as spawning grounds. During the spawning period males and females chase each other in courtship. As this involves plenty of exercise, they need to compensate for consumption of energy. Therefore, it is necessary to feed goldfish amply in summer and autumn so they can store fat in the body before the arrival of winter, when goldfish prepare for propagation the following year.

During the propagation season, give goldfish intensive care. In the daytime drain water from the tub or jar to make it shallow and give goldfish enough sunshine. At night add water to the container to maintain water temperature so that the difference in temperature between day and night does not exceed four degrees Centigrade.

If these conditions are provided, goldfish will breed normally.

Methods of Propagation

Natural Propagation   When goldfish mate and spawn spontaneously, it is called natural propagation.

When goldfish are about to spawn, put males and females of the same species in a container so that their offspring will not be a mixed species. As the water temperature rises the goldfish get excited. After a few days the male chases close behind the female, indicating the ova have matured. At this time put sterilized aguatic weeds or palm bark into the water.

At dawn the following day the male is in true hot pursuit. When the female swims near aquatic weeds,

55.

1. Female's genital aperture.
2. Male's genital aperture.

35

the male catches up with her and eagerly uses its mouth to bump against the female's belly and stimulate spawning. The female turns its genital aperture towards the aquatic weeds, trembles all over and lays eggs that adhere to the weeds. Almost at the same time the male sways its tail and ejects sperm to unite with the ova. Thus the ova become fertilized (Fig. 56).

With each tremble the female lays a small number of eggs, so the process is fairly long. In general, it begins at daybreak and continues until noon. When the female stops spawning, remove the aquatic weeds with fertilized eggs stuck to them and hatch the eggs in a jar with water of the same temperature. Separate male and female fish and feed them in different jars temporarily, so as to prevent the males from continu-

ing to chase the females and even bumping them injuring their scales and impairing their appearance.

In natural propagation males can eject sperm i only a limited space, achieving a very low fertilizatio rate of eggs.

Artificial propagation Artificial propagatio permits one to cultivate new varieties. In early morn ing, when the female is being hotly pursued by th male, immediately scoop up the female and gentl press its belly. If ova flow out, this indicates they hav matured. Stop pressing the female's belly and put th fish into another jar for one to two hours. Then scoo up the required male fish and wipe water drops from its body. With a small glass tube suck the cream

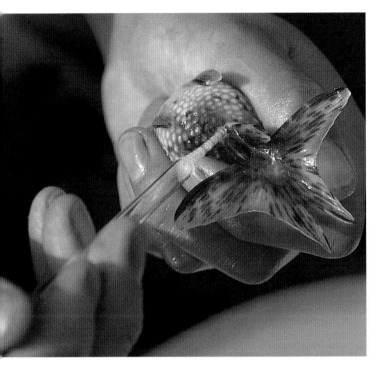

57. First step in artificial insemination—stripping fish of semen.

58. Second step in artificial insemination—stripping fish of eggs.

59. Third step in artificial insemination—the mixing of sperm and ova.

coloured semen out of the male's genital aperture and put it into a small dry glass (Fig. 57), then take the female, wipe it dry and gently press its belly so that ova flow into the glass to mix with the semen. Slowly stir them (Figs. 58, 59). Finally, pour the fertilized eggs evenly into a previously prepared pan or tub filled with fresh water. The fertilized eggs will stick firmly to the container (Fig. 60). After ten minutes drain off

the old water and pour in new. Then proceed with hatching the eggs (Fig. 61).

Hatching the Eggs

The fertilized eggs in water of 18 to 22 degrees Centigrade will hatch in five to seven days (Fig. 62, 63).

During the hatching pay attention to the following:

1) Changes in water temperature greatly influence the hatching of fertilized eggs. The optimum water

61. Hatching eggs.

emperature is 18 to 22 degrees Centigrade. If the water temperature is too high, the young, weak fry will find it difficult to adapt. If the temperature is too low, the fry will hatch slowly and be liable to suffocation and death. If the temperature is high one moment, low the next, this will also affect the emerging of fry. Thus, maintaining optimum water temperature is the key to preserving fry.

2) Avoid direct sunlight on fertilized eggs. If the sun is too strong shade the eggs with reed matting or bamboo curtain.

3) During hatching most of the yellow eggs will gradually turn black and you can see the small fish bodies coiled inside. A small number, however, will turn greyish white. These are dead eggs. Clear them out at once; otherwise the dead eggs will become mouldy, which will affect water quality and the normal hatching of the other fertilized eggs and the growth of fry.

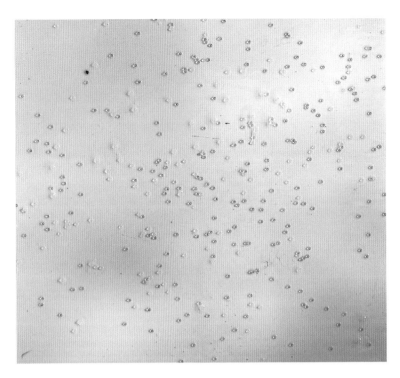

62. Ova in which the bodies of young fish have taken shape.

63. Fry that have just broken out of eggs.

64. Variegated carplike goldfish shaped like the Chinese character "𡥋" (wen).

Tending Goldfish

SOME people believe goldfish are good-looking but hard to raise. As a matter of fact, provided you create a suitable environment for them (clear water, frequent change of water, plenty of sunshine and sufficient food), you can raise them well.

Water and Food

Water and food are the basic substances for goldfish.

Water Treatment   Goldfish cannot live without water, but, it can't be just any kind of water. It must be fresh water between 10 and 30 degrees Centigrade.

Well water or tap water is generally used for rearing goldfish, but it must first be treated. Fresh tap water and well water contain insufficient oxygen for goldfish, and tap water, being sterilized, often contains more bleaching powder than goldfish can adapt to. More important is water temperature. If you put goldfish directly into water that is cold, they will breathe with difficulty, even fall ill and die.

It is necessary to bask the water in the sun and store it for a period before using it so that its temperature will be close to that of a pond. Moreover, in the process of storing tap water a large amount of bleaching powder can evaporate and oxygen be absorbed into it. Such water, after basking and storing, is the ideal environment for goldfish.

Capturing Water Fleas   Goldfish eat a wide range of food, including fish meat, silkworm larvae, shrimp skin, eggyolk, pig's blood, millet and dry noodles, but they are especially fond of water fleas.

Water fleas, which live in ponds and creeks, are small insects as red as blood. They are a common species of plankton in fresh water. Some are lower crustaceans of the order Cladocera. Such water fleas possess very high nutritional value and contain a large amount of protein in their bodies. Goldfish grow fast and fat on water fleas. Besides, cladoceran water fleas contain multiple vitamins, which give goldfish gorgeous colour. Such water fleas breed rapidly. When you discover a large number of them, catch them. You will not reduce their number but improve their pro-

AquaSafe/ContraChlorine Plus

Tetra's AquaSafe neutralizes chlorine and heavy metals, while providing goldfish with a protective coating against wounds and abrasions. ContraChlorine Plus is an ideal companion product to AquaSafe in areas where chloramine is added to the water system. Both products should be used in new aquariums and after every water change.

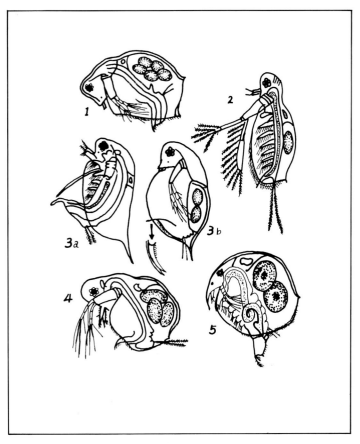

65. Common goldfish feed—Cladocera

1. Water flea (*Scapholeberis muconata*, O. F. Muller).
2. Water flea (*Diaphanosoma brachyurum*, Lievin).
3a. Water flea (*Daphnia pulex de Geer*, male).
3b. Water flea (*Daphnia pulex de Geer*, tail claws).
4. Water flea (*Moina dubia* de Guerne et Richard).
5. Water flea (*Chydorusoovalis*, Kurz).

pagation capacity (Fig. 65). Another lower crustacea of the order Copepoda (Fig. 66), is also common used to feed goldfish.

Tubifex, freshwater worms, are also food fc goldfish. When clean water flows, the tubifex's hea will emerge from the mud. Scoop it up, wash it wit fresh water and feed it to the goldfish. As it inconvenient to scoop up worms, they are not widel used.

The time and method for catching water fleas var with the particular circumstances. On clear summe days catch them in the morning, when they mov about on the water's surface. Scoop them up with net. At noon water fleas swim to the bottom, so yo have to stir the water first with the net to make th water fleas come to the surface. Then you can scoo them up. On windy days water fleas gather at leeward spot or a spot with a favourable wind in th pond, so you should search for them there.

To make the water fleas you've caught surviv

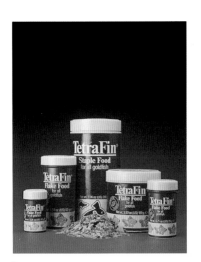

TetraFin

TetraFin Flake Food contains vital proteins and amino acids to promote color and growth.

Tetra Delica Bloodworms/Daphnia

Tetra Delica Bloodworms and Daphnia (Water Fleas) are highly nutritious foods which are an essential and well received part of the goldfish diet. Both are cleaned, dried, and packaged in sealed containers to ensure freshness and purity.

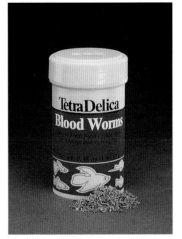

nger, swing them to reduce their moisture and let
em lie dormant temporarily. After swinging them
y, don't let them in the sun. With proper handling
ater fleas will survive for six hours.

Back home, wash the water fleas with fresh water
d remove other small insects. Then you can feed the
eas to the goldfish. If you have scooped up too many
ater fleas for one feeding, store them temporarily in
jar of fresh water. The following day scoop up living
sects on the top layer and continue to feed the
oldfish. Scald surplus water fleas with boiling water
d use them as feed after drying them in the sun.

In winter it is difficult to catch water fleas. Buy
ome sheep's or pig's blood, steam it, rub it in your
ands until pulverized, then wash it in fresh water and
se it as feed. Millet or rice, boiled and washed, can
so be used as feed for goldfish.

essels for Raising Goldfish

Choose beautifully shaped vessels to add orna-

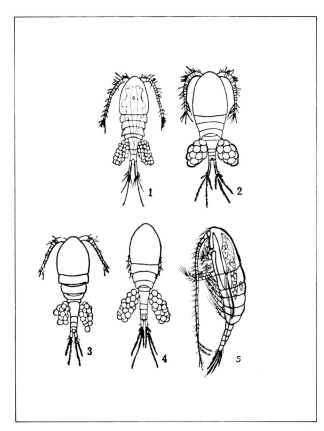

66. Common goldfish feed—Copepoda

1. Water flea (*Cyclops vicinus vicinus*).
2. *Eucyclops serrulatus*.
3. *Thermocyclops taihokuensis*.
4. *Mesocyclops leuckarti*.
5. *Calanus fimarchicus*.

mental appeal and wide-mouthed jars or tubs that permit as much water as possible to come in contact with the air and absorb oxygen. The body of the jar should not be too deep and its inner wall should be smooth so that the goldfish will not injure themselves while swimming. If raise goldfish in your home or a small courtyard, the jar should be small enough to move. In a park or other public place larger vessels can be used to make it more convenient for visitors' appreciation.

Goldfish are a living work of art. If you put a pair of attractive goldfish in a vessel of beautiful shape, you are "adding flowers to the brocade," as the saying goes. In Ming and Qing times China already had a great many exquisite vessels for goldfish. For instance,

fish basins in the Jiajing period (1522-1566) and in the Kangxi-Qianlong period (1662-1795) and tables for glass goldfish tanks in the imperial palaces of the capital were all carefully manufactured and carved out of the best materials. These centuries-old vessels are prized for their shape and colour and have become artworks of high ornamental value (Figs. 67 to 76).

Nowadays, with the raising of goldfish so popular, vessels of diverse styles have increased. Traditional Chinese vessels include earthenware jars, wooden tube, brownish-yellow sandy pottery jars, pottery jars, aquariums and glass bowls.

Earthenware Jars and Wooden Tubs Earth

67. Blue-and-white porcelain gold-fish basin made in Jiajing period (1522-1566) of the Ming Dynasty.

68, 69. White marble goldfish ba-sins (left, fragmentary) of the Kangxi-Qianlong period (1662-1795).

70. Table made of nanmu (a fine, valuable wood) in the Qing Dynas-ty (1644-1911) with a glass gold-fish tank.

71. Wooden tubs for goldfish.

enware jars and wooden tubs are common vessels fo
raising goldfish in northern China. Earthenware jar
or basins, come in many sizes and are low price
Wooden tubs are generally round or oval and mac
of wood of the arborvitae tree. These two kinds o
vessels can be used in both scenic spots and homes.

**Brownish-Yellow Sandy Pottery Jars and Ord
nary Pottery Jars**   These are widely used in souther
China. The former, wide-mouthed, are popular, lov
priced fish raising vessels. The latter are shaped lik
flowerpots, with decorative patterns carved on th
outside and smooth inner walls. When precious vari
ties of goldfish are reared in such jars, they loo
elegant and unconventional. Such goldfish jars ar
suitable for ancient buildings.

Aquariums and Glass Bowls   Aquariums ar
ideal for raising goldfish at home and for display a
goldfish exhibitions. When rockery and aquatic weed
are put in an aquarium, goldfish swim in the midst o
luxuriant verdure, giving a richer, three-dimensiona
effect. Such tanks, made of glass and a metal frame
work, have been used widely in recent years. Glas

72. Earthenware jars.

owls, smaller than aquariums, are displayed on tables
n homes.

All fish-rising containers should be put in sunny,
ell-ventilated places.

73. Pottery jars.

Raising Fry

When fry break out of the eggs, they have no
cales on their bodies. Only five millimetres long, they
dhere to the bottom of the jar or aquatic weeds and
either eat nor move about. They are very fragile;
heir bodies are transparent and their caudal and dorsal
ins have not differentiated. They live entirely on
itellus inside their bodies.

After two or three days the fry begin to swim and
earch for food. Feed them some boiled eggyolk once
very morning and evening.

Fry that have just begun to take food must be put
n shallow water five to ten centimetres deep in the

74. Brownish-yellow sandy pottery
jars.

47

sun. If you put them rather deep, wide water, they will die. If the weather changes suddenly, move the jar indoors promptly or cover it with reed matting to maintain proper water temperature and calm, stable water.

Approximately ten days later the fry grow rapidly and gradually become robust. Provide them with an adequate supply of water fleas and change the water for the first time. To change the water, screen the fry off with a fine net and siphon off two-thirds of the water. Then scoop up the remaining water and the fry and put them in another basin. Wash the original basin clean and pour fresh water that has already basked in the sun into it. Then slowly pour the reserved fry and water into the fresh water.

After twenty days the fry's caudal fin basicall takes shape. At thirty days its body will be 1. centimetres long and you can tell whether or not i caudal fin is good. Its body colour also become apparent if it is to be variegated, purple or blue Goldfish that will finally be red or black, howeve remain bluish grey. Keep fry with good body shap and widespread caudal fin and eliminate the others.

When the young fish are two centimetres lon they swim faster and grow more quickly. They nee more food and are always searching for it. If you don feed them in time, they will kill one another out c hunger.

It is necessary to add a small amount of fresh wate

Aquariums.

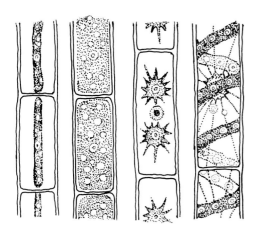

77. Green moss good for fry.

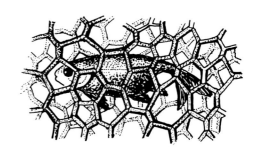

78. Fry trapped by netlike algae.

to the fish pond or jar every day to conserve adequate oxygen in the water and let the young fish grow up healthy. In the early period of raising fry, as the water temperature reaches 18 to 20 degrees Centigrade, green moss and netlike algae grow quickly. When the fry swim into them, their bodies get entangled (Figs. 77, 78). When you find plenty of green moss and netlike algae in the water, remove them and change the water.

Harmful insects often mingle with the water fleas you scoop up. The water centipede (larva of Cybister, Fig. 79), one of them, imposes a great menace to young fish. It is a carnivorous aquatic insect and uses its sharp clamps to squeeze the fish to death. Before

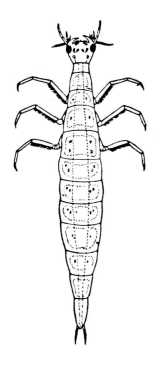

79. Water centipede, larva of Cybister species, is a carnivorous aquatic insect. It first squeezes the fry to death, then eats it.

eding the fry water fleas, sift them to remove water ntipedes and other harmful insects.

After two months or so the young fish, in general, row to at least four centimetres. At this time choose gain, keeping fish with gorgeous colours, symmetri- al shapes and prominent characteristics to be bred as rnamental or stock fish.

ending Adult Fish

Generally goldfish live five to six years, ten years t most. Their age can be determined by the rings on heir scales. When you put a scale under a microscope, you can see concentric circles, one for each year of the fish's life (Figs. 80, 81). To prolong goldfish's life, attention should be paid to the following:

1) Changing water. The purpose of changing the water is to keep it clean, regulate the temperature and increase the oxygen content in order to provide a favourable environment for the growth of goldfish.

There are two methods of changing water. One is to change all the water; scoop up all the fish and move them to water that has basked in the sun. When algae in the water have multiplied enormously or when the pond water has deteriorated, you must adopt this method. The other method is to change part of the

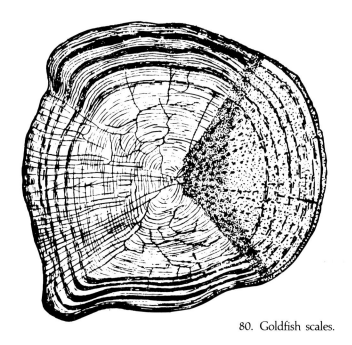

80. Goldfish scales.

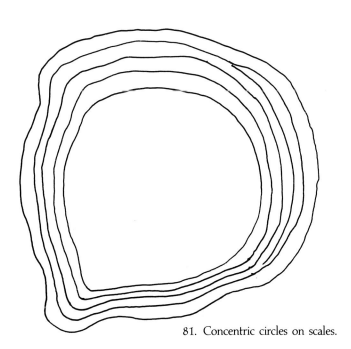

81. Concentric circles on scales.

water; siphon off a third or half the water, replace it with fresh water that has basked in the sun (Fig. 82).

The time for changing water varies with the seasons. In spring, since the temperature changes little, it is necessary to remove only a part of the old water and replenish it with new. Change the water at nine a.m. or three p.m. every day.

In summer and autumn water should be change after four p.m. If you stir up the water at noon, whe the sunshine is intense and the water temperatur high, the fishes' growth will be affected. You must ad new water and remove unwanted matter every day t

82. Siphoning off old water.

void the disintegration of alien matter and the consumption of oxygen. If the water is deficient in
oxygen, the fish will inhale oxygen from the air. This
called head afloat, and it lasts too long, the goldfish
will die. If you notice heads afloat, immediately pour
fresh water into the pond or jar.

Indoor vessels are usually small and hold only a
small amount of water, so it is easy for water quality
to deteriorate, especially in the summer, when goldfish
swim more than usual and quickly consume the
oxygen in the water. Since there is no sunshine
indoors, the oxygen cannot be replenished. Most
goldfish raised indoors have their heads afloat in the
morning. This is the main cause for higher mortality
among goldfish raised indoors. Only by increasing the
frequency of changing the water, artificially providing
a favourable environment for goldfish, can you ensure
adequate oxygen in the water and reduce goldfish
mortality.

When changing water in summer and autumn,
remember that goldfish are cold-blooded creatures, so

83. Scooping up goldfish: Scoop
from head to rear to avoid impairing fish's scales.

their body temperature rises and falls with that of the outside world. If the water temperature drops suddenly when you change the water, causing an abrupt temperature change, the goldfish will find it difficult to adapt. When swimming, they will appear restless and their bodies will be covered with small drops of water, indicating they have caught cold. Move them to water of the same temperature as formerly and a short time later they will return to normal.

"Tail burning" also occurs easily in summer and autumn, when green algae multiply enormously and the sunshine causes them to release too much oxygen in the water. In tail burning the goldfish's fins are obviously congested and are covered with transparent bubbles. The fish becomes too sluggish to swim; its head hangs down and its caudal fins float on the surface. When you notice such a symptom, at once move the goldfish to fresh water of appropriate temperature. Two or three days later the congestion will disappear, the small bubbles will break up and the goldfish will be lively again. Changing the water every day is the principal method for preventing tail burning.

In winter the interval for changing water may b longer, three or four days for changing part of th water and every half month for changing all the wate As for goldfish wintering outdoors, when the wat temperature drops below zero degrees Centigrade ar there is a thin layer of ice on the water, their everyda life is not affected. Just break up the ice to avoid i thickening and to replenish oxygen.

2) Catching goldfish. Goldfish are loved f their gorgeous colours and beautiful shapes, so i catching them you must not impair their appearanc

Sometimes you have to scoop goldfish up t change their water, and it's easy to injure then especially the female, whose scales are fairly loose an can fall off if hit. Impaired, a goldfish loses i ornamental value; moreover, bacteria will take th chance to enter its body. Therefore, in scooping it u cast the net along its head towards the rear so the ne follows the direction of the scales and does not injur the fish (Fig. 83). After scooping up the goldfish, pu it into water immediately to avoid its heaping in th net. If a goldfish's scales do get knocked off, they wil row again after some time. If goldfish are injured, put them in a solution of a small amount of water and salt or bleaching powder, soak them a short while, then return them to their pond. Such sterilization will guard against infection.

3) Feeding and tending. In spring goldfish, having survived the winter, need to regain their vitality and prepare for spawning. Therefore, you should give them fresh feed to meet their needs. Give them just the right amount, so it will be eaten up within three or four hours. It is also important to protect stock fish against disease during the fishes' propagating season.

Although summer and autumn are the seasons when goldfish develop, sometimes such factors as intense sunshine, deficiency of oxygen and abnormal weather changes menace their growth. Therefore, it is necessary to give intensive care to the goldfish. Feeding should be at regular hours and in regular quantities. Feed them in the morning and afternoon every day. Vary the amount of feed according to the size of the fish, not giving too much. It is best if the feed is eaten up within two to three hours.

In winter, with the lowering of the water temperature, goldfish wintering outdoors swim less and are not eager to search for food. Sometimes they lie motionless at the bottom of the water, almost in a state of hibernation. At this time goldfish subsist mainly on the fat stored during summer and autumn. When the water temperature drops below five degrees Centigrade, you can feed them little or no food without much effect on their lives. As for goldfish wintering indoors, if the water temperature remains above five degrees Centigrade, it is necessary to feed them water fleas every day, replenish some of the water every two or three days, and often put the fish in sunlight. Otherwise, goldfish will gradually become emaciated.

One problem in raising goldfish is that sometimes the colour will fade or not change for a long time. The goldfish's colour has a direct relationship to the intensity of the sun's rays. For instance, the red goldfish is bluish grey when it breaks out of the egg. Raised outdoors, it begins to change colour after about three months. First, its body turns black, then its belly turns yellow; the yellow spreads upward and gradually becomes red. If there is not enough light, the colour

84. For a long journey, put fish i[n] plastic bag, fill bag with oxyge[n] then put bag in box.

change will be delayed. If a goldfish that has already turned red lives long in an environment without sunshine, its colour will fade. If goldfish raised indoors fail to change colour when they should, the cause is precisely too little sunshine. Therefore, whether outdoors or indoors, goldfish need plenty of sunshine so they can maintain their gorgeous colours and high ornamental value.

4) How to travel with goldfish. To travel with goldfish, use a bucket or a plastic bag. For a short trip a bucket will suffice, but take care not to put too many fish in the bucket. On the way if you discover heads are afloat (goldfish putting their mouths out of th[e] water to inhale oxygen), add fresh water to the bucke[t.] For a long journey it's usually best to use a plastic ba[g.] The day preceding departure stop feeding the fish. A[t] the time of departure fill one-fifth of the plastic ba[g] with water, then put an appropriate number of gold[-] fish into it. Pump air from the bag, insert an oxyge[n] tube into it and slowly fill it with oxygen until it swell[s] up. Take out the tube, firmly bind the mouth of th[e] plastic bag with a rubber band and put the bag into [a] box. Now you can start your journey (Fig. 84). For [a] short trip it is not necessary to fill the plastic wit[h] oxygen.

Prevention and Treatment
of Fish Diseases

THE study, prevention and treatment of fish diseases began very early in China. Su Shi, a famous essayist and poet of the Song Dynasty (960-1279), wrote in *A Manual on the Mutual Influence of Things,* "When a fish becomes emaciated and white spots appear on its body, we call this ailment fish louse. If you put a maple twig into the water, the fish will be cured." Over the past several decades China has achieved great success and gained rich experience in the study, prevention and treatment of fish diseases.

Causes for the Occurrence of Disease

The cleanness of the water is an important factor in determining whether or not goldfish will fall ill. If water is polluted by bacteria, the bacteria often penetrate any injury on a goldfish's body or live as parasites in its body and breed enormously. If a goldfish is in good condition and has some resistance, its ailment will heal without treatment after a time. If a goldfish is fragile, it will not be able to resist bacteria and will fall ill. Common diseases are mostly caused by contamination of fungi and bacteria or the onslaught of parasites. These pathogenic bacteria and parasites are mainly brought in when scooping up water fleas. Therefore, before putting water fleas into the fish water, be sure to wash them with fresh water. In this way you will efficiently prevent goldfish from falling ill.

Methods for Examining
Fish Diseases

It is not easy to diagnose fish diseases. Generally you can determine them only through the fish's external manifestations.

Most sick goldfish have poor appetites, swim slowly and are dull in colour. If such symptoms occur, promptly examine the fish. Scoop it up into a smaller vessel and examine whether or not there are large pathogens on the body. If you see none with the naked eye, you can guess from the symptoms or make a microscopic examination. The next step is to examine the fish's gills. Gently hold the fish in one hand and open the gill cover with your other hand. Generally a goldfish's gill filaments are bright red, but when a fish falls ill, its gill filaments turn white or grey and become fragmentary. You can diagnose the fish's disease after examination and prescribe medicines accordingly (Fig. 85).

Preparation and Use of Medicines

The medicines used for treating goldfish disease are mostly poisonous or corrosive. Therefore, you must prepare them accurately according to the required concentration. First weigh the drug and prepare a highly concentrated solution. When you use the medicine, add water to dilute it to the required concentration.

85. Examining the gills.

86. Goldfish suffering from white spot disease.

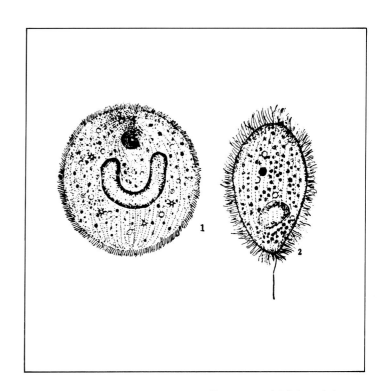

87. Protozoan of Ichthyophthirius, which causes white spot disease

1. Adult insect.
2. Larva.

The best method for treating fish diseases is ~aking. Put the sick fish into the prepared medicinal ~quid and soak it awhile, observing it all the time. The ~aked fish should then be put into clean, fresh water ~ recuperate.

The concentration of the medicinal liquid depends on the fish's size and physique and the warmth of the water temperature. To treat a small, fragile goldfish, use a small dose of medicinal liquid and high water temperature and soak the fish for a short period; to treat a large fish with strong physique, use a large dose of medicinal liquid and low water temperature and soak the fish for a long time.

GoldOomed

Tetra Medica GoldOomed is a broad range, non-antibiotic treatment for both parasitic and bacterial diseases afflicting all goldfish, and is ideal for protecting and treating exotic goldfish. Safe, reliable, and easy to use.

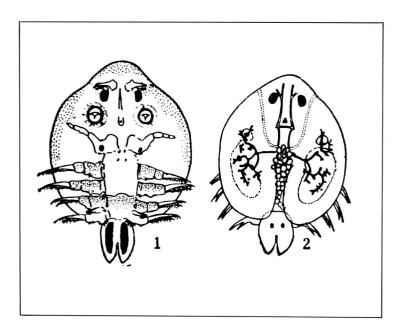

88. Pathogens of fish louse disease

1. Male.
2. Back of female.

Methods for Treating Several Common Diseases

White Spot Disease White spot disease (a disease caused by insects of Ichthyophthirius, Fig. 86) is caused by protozoans of Ichthyophthirius that live as parasites on the fish's body. This disease is extremely detrimental to goldfish. The fish will have white cysts covered with white mucus all over its body and gills. It gradually becomes emaciated, swims slowly and sometimes floats motionless on the surface and dies a few days later. The protozoans absorb cell fluid as nutrition from the tissues of the goldfish's body, causing necrosis of the tissues and the fish's death. The disease is most rampant and detrimental when the water temperature ranges between 20 and 30 degrees Centigrade (Fig. 87).

Method of treatment: Soak the fish in a solutic of two parts per million of mercurous nitrate at temperature of 20 degrees Centigrade for twenty t forty minutes. Do not soak in direct sunlight or in metal basin. The soaking should kill the parasites.

Fish Louse Disease The fish louse is a species c parasite. It can live on different parts of the goldfish body (Fig. 88). Fish louse disease mostly occurs in Jun and July every year. The fish louse uses its stinger an palate to scrape the goldfish's skin and suck its bloo While doing so, it inflicts many wounds and cause the skin to inflame and rot. A goldfish suffering fror is disease often twists and wriggles restlessly close to the water's surface. Some die of the disease.

Method of treatment: Scoop up the fish with parasitic lice on their bodies and soak them in a solution of one part per fifty thousand of dipterex at a temperature of about 25 degrees Centigrade for fifteen to twenty minutes. This will kill all the fish lice.

Water Mould (Fig. 89)   Water mould is caused by fungi. It occurs mainly in spring, with a small number of cases in other seasons.

Spots where a fish's scales have fallen off and wounds are susceptible to the penetration of water mould fungi. As soon as the fungi enter, many woolly or furry substances, visible to the naked eye, adhere

89. Goldfish suffering from water mould, raised in basin.

to the wounds and rapidly spread all over the body. Water mould fungi absorb nutrients from the fish's body and breed enormously. This burdens the goldfish and produces abnormal movement. Water mould fungus in the gills seals the gill cover and affects the fish's breathing, causing it to suffocate and die.

Method of treatment: Soak fish in one part per hundred thousand of malachite soaking solution at a temperature of 15 to 20 degrees Centigrade for ten to fifteen minutes. This will cure the fish of water mould, but the best method is to prevent water mould by keeping the water clean, removing any unwanted matter promptly. Thus water mould fungus cannot grow and multiply.

Bacterial Gill Rot (Fig. 90) The fish's gill filaments turn white and become fragmentary. Some rot and bleeding appears on the epidermis of the gill cover. The sick fish moves slowly, floats on the water breathes with difficulty and finally suffocates to death. The fish has been infected with mucoglobular bacteria which mostly occurs when water quality has deteriorated. Gill rot spreads very easily. As soon as you discover such symptoms, isolate the sick fish, feed it fewer water fleas and change the water often to prevent spread of the bacteria.

Method of treatment: Soak the fish in a solution of one part per hundred thousand of bleaching powder for ten minutes, then move it to new water. Soak

90. Goldfish suffering from gill rot and a sample of rotten gills.

Goldfish suffering from scale-erect disease.

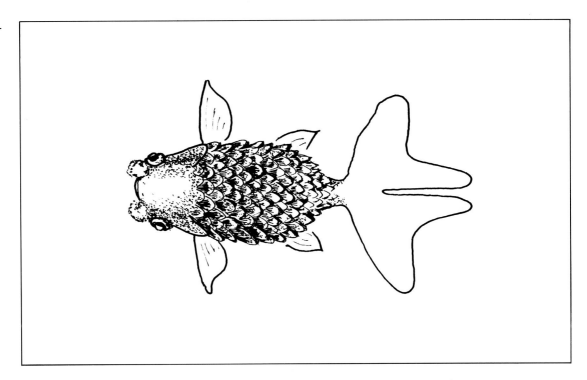

again two days later and move it to new water to recuperate. It will recover in a few days.

Scale-erect Disease (Fig. 91)   The scales on the sick fish's body stand erect so that the whole body resembles an opening pine cone. When you squeeze the scales, fluid will spurt out and scales fall off.

Scale-erect disease occurs mostly in winter or early spring. When the fish falls ill, bleeding appears on its epidermis and its eyes protrude. As the ailment progresses, the fish is unable to swim and it flips over, belly upward. Bacteria enter the body mainly through wounds, so when scooping up fish, take care not to bruise them. If you do not give the sick fish prompt treatment, it will die within a few days.

Method of treatment: Move fish that have just fallen sick to new water and they will recover within a few days. In severe cases soak fish in a solution of 2 percent sodium chloride and 3 percent sodium bicarbonate at a temperature of 10 degrees Centigrade for five to ten minutes, then move fish to new water. A few days later the sick fish will swim at ease and their scales gradually return to normal.

Gyrodactylus Disease   The body of a goldfish suffering severely from the disease caused by the Gyrodactylus insect loses its original lustre and develops a layer of greyish-white mucous membrane. The fish swims restlessly, has a poor appetite, becomes emaciated, breathes with difficulty and finally dies.

The Gyrodactylus insect belongs to the catego[ry] of sucking insects (Fig. 92). It lives as a parasite on th[e] goldfish's body and fins, sucking epidemic tissues an[d] mucus from the fish's body. When a goldfish h[as] insufficient feed or suffers from malnutrition, it [is] susceptible to the disease.

Method of treatment: Soak the fish in a soluti[on] of two parts per hundred thousand of potassiu[m] permanganate for fifteen to twenty minutes at a tim[e.]

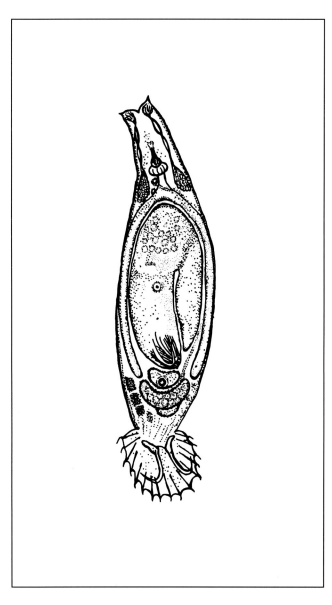

92. Gyrodactylus insect.

Goldfish in Ponds and Pools

To successfully keep goldfish in outdoor ponds and pools, use AquaSafe Pond Formula to immediately neutralize chlorine, chloramine and heavy metals, while providing a protective coating for the gills and membranes of your pond fish.

Tetra DesaFin combines formaldehyde and malachite green to both prevent and treat a broad range of parasitic and bacterial diseases which commonly afflict pool and pond kept goldfish.

93. Red dragon eyes.

Red dragon eyes have been raised [in] China for nearly three hundred yea[rs.] They are bright red with protruding ey[e-] balls and thin, widespread caudal fi[ns.] This variety of fish, with good adaptati[on] and a fondness for sunshine, is ideal [for] raising at home. Ones with symmetri[c] eyeballs are regarded as a superb variet[y.] An adult fish measures between 15 a[nd] 25 cm.

Introduction to Goldfish Varieties

GENERALLY the goldfish has a short, plump body with three or four caudal fins. It is red, orange, purple, black, blue, silvery white or variegated in colour. Over the long course of breeding and artificial selection many varieties have been created. They consist approximately of three categories: firstly, carplike varieties, with powerful fins and crossed caudal fins, such as goose head and pearl scales. They are shaped like the Chinese character "文" (*wen*), meaning literature. Secondly, dragon varieties with two bulging eyes and well-developed fins, such as dragon eyes. Thridly, egg-shaped varieties without a dorsal fin, such as velvet balls, tiger head, bubble eyes and egg shape with phoenix tail (with large, beautiful and widespread caudal fins).

94, 95. Purple dragon eyes with red balls

An unusual variety of goldfish, It is deep purple all over and its mouth is flanked by two bright-red velvet balls. An adult fish measures 17 cm.

96. Red dragon eyes with high head

This goldfish has a square, solid, helmet-like shape on its head with bulges around its eyeballs. Its caudal fins are large and widespread. An adult fish measures between 18 and 20 cm.

97. Variegated butterfly tail with reversed gills.

98. Black butterfly tail with bulging dragon eyes

An exceedingly rare variety of goldfish, renowned for its butterflylike caudal fins. It is as black as traditional Chinese ink and has large, protruding eyes. This variety of fish likes shallow water, only 10 cm deep. An adult fish measures between 15 and 20 cm.

99. Black pearl scales with bulging dragon eyes

A recent variety of extremely small number. Its black body is covered with pearl scales in neat array. Eyes are also black. An adult fish measures between 15 and 18 cm.

100. Red-and-white pearl scales with dragon eyes.

101. Red dragon eyes with crane crest.

102. Dragon eyes with balls and black-and-white magpielike patterns.

103. Purple-and-blue dragon eyes with high head.

104. Black-and-red dragon eyes with balls and reversed gills.

105. Dragon back with red tiger head

This fish has a short, sturdy body and no dorsal fin. Its protruding eyeballs are hemmed in by bulges. A helmetlike shape on the crest resembles an inlaid gem. This variety likes to swim on the bottom. An adult fish measures between 12 and 15 cm.

106. Dragon back with red head.

107. Sky-gazing eyes with red balls

A rare variety. Its two eyes gaze skyward and the two velvet balls in front of the eyeballs resemble two fresh flowers. The variety was artificially crossbred in recent years. Today there are only a few, seen in only a few areas. An adult fish measures 15 cm.

Variegated sky-gazing eyes.

Purple sky-gazing eyes

[A]ll varieties with sky-gazing eyes this [is th]e most precious. Its shape is beautiful [and] its colour deep and gorgeous. In [devel]oping, it is fairly difficult for its [eyeb]alls to take shape. When selecting, [pick] one with symmetrical eyeballs turn[ing] upward at an angle of 90 degrees. [Only] such a fish is superb. An adult fish [meas]ures 12 cm.

Red-and-white   sky-gazing [eyes].

11. Red sky-gazing bubble eyes

[T]his fish's eyeballs turn upward and are [e]mbedded in two tremulous bubbles. The [v]ariety is the result of artificial cross-[b]reeding. The fish is easy to raise. In [s]electing, pick one with large soft bubbles [a]nd symmetrical upward-turning eyeballs. [O]nly such a fish is of excellent variety. [A]n adult fish measures between 15 and [1]7 cm.

112. Red crane crest

One of the most precious varieties
goldfish. It is silvery white all over wi
a red bulge on its head; it swims as if
were a crane dancing. As early as t
Ming Dynasty (1368-1644) there we
red-crested goldfish. At that time t
species had only a red spot instead of
bulge on top of the head. This fish
delicate in temperament and should
fed separately. An adult fish measur
between 20 and 25 cm.

3. Jadestone seal on head.

114. Jade seal impression on head

This fish is golden red all over. At the upper end of a bulge on the head is a square light-yellow shape, resembling the impression of a beautiful jade seal. In selecting, choose one with a square, solid bulge on the head and no mottled spots on its body. Only such a fish is of top grade. An adult fish measures between 17 and 21 cm.

115. Variegated fish with red high head.

This variety has the following characteristics: head covered with small bright-red bulges leading down to the cheeks; only the eyeballs are black. It is costly because of its gorgeous colour, and it is prized as a treasure. An adult fish measures between 18 and 20 cm.

6. Red-and-white high head.

117. Balls with high head, reversed gills and black-and-white magpielike patterns

A new variety bred in recent years. Its black-and-white pattern resembles the plumage of a magpie. Bulges grow all over the top of the head. The gill covers are reversed, showing bright-red gill filaments. Two small velvetlike balls grow at its nostrils. An adult fish measures between 17 and 19 cm.

8. Blue high head.

119. Variegated balls with high head.

120. Purple balls with high head.

121. Red balls with high head.

122. Red high head.

123. Purple pearl scales

This variety has a belly as round as a ball and its deep-purple scales are as lustrous as pearls. It is lively by nature and likes to swim about. An adult fish measures 15 cm.

124. Red pearl scales with reversed gills

This variety has a pointed head and round belly. The gill filaments—bright, sparkling, gorgeous colour—on each side of the head are revealed. An adult fish measures 14 cm.

125. Variegated pearl scales

This variety has a pointed head and a small tail and its belly resembles a ball so it is also called rubber-ball pearl. It scales, prominent in the centre, scintillate It is prized as a treasure among goldfish Variegated pearl-scales are suitable fo raising in shallow water in a smooth vessel. Since the scales fall off easily, take care in raising them. When selecting choose one with a full round belly, scale in neat array and evenly distributed spot of diverse colours. Only such a fish is o top grade. An adult fish measures be tween 12 and 18 cm.

6. Variegated lion head

is variety has solid bulges all over the head with eyes
d mouth embedded in the bulges. It has a broad back
thout dorsal fin and a short, widespread tail. This fish
es to swim with other goldfish at the lower level of
allow water. In selecting, ones with the most devel-
ed bulges are best. An adult fish measures 15 cm.

7. Lion head with cinnabar eyes.

128. Red-and-white lion head.

129. Red tiger head.

130. Tiger head with white pearl scales

A new variety bred in recent years. Its head is covered all over with bulges and the scales on its body resemble lustrous pearls. It swims steadily and likes to be with other goldfish. An adult fish measures 12 cm.

131. Red goose head

A famous variety. A bright-red lump of flesh decorates the top of the head. It has no dorsal fin. Its caudal fins are short and solid, and its short, big belly resembles a duck egg. An adult fish measures 13 cm.

132. Variegated frog head

This variety is known as such because it head is broad, flat and triangular like frog's head. Gorgeous in colour, it ha ornamental value. An adult fish measure 16 cm.

133. Red frog head with reversed gills.

. Red frog head with pearl
es.

. Red frog head with pearl
es and reversed gills

new variety artificially crossbred in
nt years. Judging by its appearance, it
tually a combination of red frog head
reversed gills and red frog head with
l scales. An adult fish measures
cm.

136. White bubble eyes with goose head.

137. Bubble eyes with hoisted fins and black-and-white magpielike pattern.

138. Red bubbles.

A precious variety, renowned for the two fiery red bubbles underneath the eyes. In has a gentle temperament and likes to shuttle back and forth on the bottom, so keep the water clean at the bottom of the tub or jar. When changing water and scooping the fish up, avoid bumping the bubbles. Once the bubbles break, they cannot regenerate. When selecting, choose ones with large, symmetrical bubbles. Only such fish are of top grade. An adult fish measures 16 cm.

139. Purple-and-blue bubble eyes with goose head and hoisted fins.

140. Red bubble eyes with goose head.

141. Cinnabar bubble eyes

This variety is silvery white all over. Only the two bubbles are red. It is a precious variety, carefully bred; only a small number exist. In selecting, choose ones with a white body and bright-red bubbles, without mottled spots on its body. Only such fish are of excellent variety. An adult fish measures 13 cm.

143. Black bubble eyes.

142. Red-and-white bubble eyes.

144. Blue bubble eyes.

45. Variegated egg shape with reversed gills.

146. Blue reversed gills.

147. Red reversed gills

The edges of the gill covers on each side of this fish turn outward, showing the bright-red gill filaments. Its body resembles a duck egg. It has no dorsal fin. This variety adapts well and has a long life. When selecting, choose ones with gill filaments revealed; the most revealed are the best. An adult fish measures 18 cm.

148. Variegated egg shape with four balls on the forehead.

149. Blue egg shape with ball

This variety has two small velvety balls at the mouth. Its colours are very sensitive to environmental changes. If you move it to a new environment, its colour will become silvery grey. Only after a period of adaptation will it regain its normal deep-blue colour. An adult fish measures 15 cm.

150. Purple egg shape with balls.

151. Red egg shape with balls.

152. White egg shape with balls.

153. Egg shape with red head and balls.

154. Red lion head with balls.

155. Red-and-white egg shape with balls.

156. Red velvet balls

A precious variety. In front of its mouth are two velvety balls. Its dorsal fin stands erect and its flat caudal fins hang down. This fish has a gentle temperament. In raising it take care to protect the two velvet balls. An adult fish measures between 15 and 17 cm.

157. Red balls with reversed gills.

158. White balls with reversed gills.

59. Red balls with dragon eyes.

0. Blue egg shape with balls and
oenix tail

amous variety. It has a short body and
g caudal fins. When it swims, its vel-
balls flutter with the water current
d complement the blue colour all over
body, looking elegant and distin-
shed. An adult fish measures 15 cm.

161. Red egg shape with balls,
phoenix tail and reversed gills.

2. Variegated egg shape with
ls and phoenix tail.

163. Red egg shape with phoenix
tail.

164. Variegated egg shape w
phoenix tail

This variety resembles a duck egg. It
no dorsal fin and its caudal fins are v
developed, generally three-fifths of
body length. The fish is fairly quiet a
likes to swim slowly. An adult fish me
ures 22 cm.

About the Author

Li Zhen, born in 1954, is a native of Xi'an, Shaanxi Province. He has specialized in the scientific research of goldfish in Xi'an Parks and Gardens Administration and published such writings as "The Raising of Goldfish," "Flowers Blossoming in Water," "The Development of Eye Patterns of Goldfish and Their Significance" and "Water Mould of Goldfish and the Method of Healing." The research project "Initial Exploration of the Classification of Varieties of Chinese Goldfish" won him an award from Shaanxi Provincial Achievements of Science and Technology.

Editor: Yan Qiubai
Photographers: Wang Ling,
                 Shi Dianbin
Design: Yu Bingnan,
                 Yan Xinqiang
Translator: Ouyang Caiwei